T0197551

Print information available on the last page

Rev. date: 06/03/2015

To order additional copies of this book, contact:
Xlibris
1-888-795-4274
www.Xlibris.com
Orders@Xlibris.com

Monty's mother picked him up from school, and on the way home Monty asked, "Can we go to the park, please?"

"No, Monty! I'm too tired," replied his mother.

"But I'm not tired," said Monty.

"Well I am," replied his mother.

"Oh, come on! Let's just go for five minutes," said Monty.

"The last time I took you to the park, you didn't want to leave when I asked you to, and you gave me a very hard time; you kept on saying, 'Five more minutes, five more minutes,'" replied his mother.

"I promise when you say let's go home, I will be ready this time," said Monty.

"I have an idea. Let's go home. You will do your homework while I prepare dinner; I will take you to the park on Saturday, and you can play for a long time, much longer than five minutes," said Monty's mother.

"Okay," Monty said in a soft voice. Monty wasn't too excited because he wanted to go to the park that very moment.

Monty and his mother went home. After Monty washed his hands, his mother offered him a piece of fruit. Everything was going as planned. Monty was doing his homework, and his mother was preparing dinner.

After a while Monty shouted excitedly, "I finished my homework!"

"That's great! Let me take a look at it to see if you made any mistakes," said his mother.

"Do you have to?" asked Monty. "Yes, Monty, I have to. It's my job. Don't worry. If there are any mistakes, we will correct them together." A short time later she said, "Wow! Excellent! You did a good job. There are no mistakes."

"Since I'm done with my homework, can I play with my Legos, please?" asked Monty. "Yes, until dinner is ready," replied his mother. Monty was very happy with his mother's response.

After playing for a short while, Monty heard his mother's voice calling, "Monty!"

He didn't answer.

"Mon-tyyy!"

"Yes, Mom!"

"Dinner is ready!" said his mother.

"I'm not hungry," replied Monty.

"But it's dinnertime, Monty!" replied his mother.

"I just started playing with my Legos; when I'm done I'll come and eat," said Monty.

"Monty, please put away the Legos," replied his mother. In a sad voice Monty said, "All right."

Monty and his mother were eating at the dinner table. With his mouth full, Monty asked his mother if he could watch television after dinner. Monty's mother agreed that he could do so after he took a bath and brushed his teeth. Once again, Monty was very happy.

Monty's mother was trying to keep a conversation going with him by asking Monty about his day at school, but Monty was busy putting spoonsful of food in his mouth and eating very quickly so he could have more time to watch television.

"It's bath time, Monty!" said his mom.

"I'll be right there," replied Monty.

It was a school night, and it was Monty's bedtime, but he was still watching television.

"It is time to go night-night, Monty," his mother said. "I need five more minutes! My show is almost over!" replied Monty. "Okay, Monty—five more minutes,"   replied his mother.

After a while, Monty heard his mother's voice.

"Time's up, Monty!"

"But I need five more minutes," replied Monty.

"You said that ten minutes ago," said Monty's mother.

"This other show just started, and it is my favorite," said Monty.

"Monty, it's way past your bedtime, and it's a school night. Please turn the television off and get into bed so you can get a good night's rest and wake up early in the morning to get to school on time," said Monty's mother.

"I don't need a good night's rest. I'm not even tired. I promise I'll wake up early tomorrow morning to get to school on time. I just need five more minutes, and then I'll be ready for bed," replied Monty.

Monty's mom walked over and turned the television off.

"Hey! That's not fair! I was watching that!" shouted Monty.

"I will let you stay up late and watch television on Friday and Saturday when it's not a school night," replied his mother.

"I never get what I want," said Monty. "You cannot always get what you want, Monty!" replied his mother.

Monty was in bed, and while his mother was tucking him in, he asked politely, "Mom, can you please read me a book?"

"Sure! Which book would you like me to read to you?" asked Monty's mother.

The Boy Who Needs Five More Minutes," said Monty.

"I don't have that one. What is your second choice?" asked Monty's mother.

In a tired voice Monty said, "Mom, please tell me a story with a happy ending!"

"I can do that! The name of my story is, `The Boy Who Always Asks for Five More Minutes,'" his mother replied.

"Is that a story about me?" asked Monty.

"No, Monty! The little boy in this story lives with his dad," replied Monty's mother.

Monty's mother began telling him a story about a boy who lived with his dad and who always asked his dad for more time to play and watch television.

Monty didn't know how the story ended because he fell fast asleep.